FROM A WOMAN'S HEART

From a Woman's Heart

By

JUDITH N. MATTISON

Illustrations by

THELMA BUSH STUBSTAD

AUGSBURG PUBLISHING HOUSE
Minneapolis   **Minnesota**

From a Woman's Heart

Copyright © 1969 Augsburg Publishing House

Library of Congress Catalog Card No. 77-84804

Manufactured in the United States of America

"...and they'll know
we are Christians
by our love."

Contents

9

A WOMAN RESPONDS

...TO OTHERS

Touch

If my life would be
Eternal,
I must touch the man
Beside me.
Clasp the hand,
Feel the pulse,
Reach beyond the outer shell
Into the depths of
Human Soul.
Give to them who would have
Meaning
The identity of being
By the basic sense
Of being touched.
Place my hand in his
To welcome,
With no haste to draw away.
Wrap my arm around
His shoulder—
Demonstrate my sympathy.
Share my smile or
Let my tears
Flow,
Falling warm upon his face.
For, like children,
Man desires
Opportunity to feel.
If my life would be
Eternal,
I must touch,
And make life real.

Revelation

Just when I was thinking
I was right, dear Lord, she showed me
That I hadn't seen the truth of things at all.

Your plan of life brings changes,
Constant growth, and opportunities
To learn from people everywhere I go.

Non-Verbal Communication

She looks at me and does not smile.
I think she must be thinking
I am foolish.
I shall be silent, for her eyes
Would seem to say that she knows better.
I dare not risk
Her stare.

But I must look beyond her outward features.
Perhaps her face would smile
If freed from fear.
Her silence may not be my condemnation,
But respect.
And I *must* risk
Her stare,
If I would care.

Plea

You know my heart rate,
Two one-thousandths, sixty-four.
You do not
Know my heart.
You see my form,
My height, my breadth.
You do not know
My depth.
My voice is in your concept,
But within me lies my soul.
Know my all;
My pain, my joy, my fear, my hope.
Know more than my exposed veneer.
Know me.

Anguish

Lonely and afraid
She stands in burning heat of
Guilt and self-reproach,
Longing for the peace of God,
The acceptance of men,
The knowledge of self.

    Give her tears to cool the fever,
    Give her rest to ease the pain.
    Give her love to soothe the chafe
    Of futile self-rejection.
    Let this fire not consume her.
    Think on her, O Lord.

Grandma Nelson

When I was a little girl
Grandma played piano
And we sang.
We sang of waves and nightcaps
And of little birds
And God.

Yesterday I held my
Grandma's hand.
It is soft and vibrant
Though she just turned eighty-two.
Yesterday we talked together
Of the mystery of life
And dying.
Grandma knows that she will die.
She is glad for her long life.
But she says that somehow
There is still so much to do.

She squeezed my hand.
She knows I love her
And that someday
I will miss her so.
But because of Grandma
I have memories—which sing
Of waves and nightcaps,
Little birds,
And God.

Friendship

She didn't say it,
But I saw it in her shaking hand.
I saw her say,
"My husband doesn't seem to understand."
And so I told her, as we talked,
About the frightening time my marriage shook,
When we had reached a hill we could not climb.

Another's sigh said, "Listen please,
I need to share this guilt.
Help me confess
So I can break the wall that it has built."
And so I asked her,
"Do you blame yourself?" and she began.
She knew that I would not condemn
Nor tell another man.

God help me to be open
And to share this honest way.
For I, too, need such friendship
As I live from day to day.

Empathy

Help me to see
That for you to be you,
You will never
Be like me.

Mother

Mother had a very lovely face,
A quiet voice.
Her skin was somehow
Softer to my touch than any other.
Suddenly, tonight I see it!
She was kind—
Her eyes were gentle.
And her smile—
How I did love to feel
Her smile upon me.
She was comfort.
I believe
She really cared about me.
Tonight she seems so very present.
(She was too young to have died.)
Through my tears tonight
I miss my mother.

Strangers

The man on the street
Was crying,
And I wondered, "Why?"
He walked alone.
Was he lonely?
Would that make him cry?
Might it help if
I stopped to listen,
Rather than driving by?
But I knew I would not
Help the stranger.
I would not try.
And I wondered, "Why?"

My Pastor

Woven sturdily of
Simple fabric,
Striving to be humble,
Shy of praise.
Emotionally bound to
Natural beauty and the past—
Creative in the visions
Of a church's changing face.
Most of all a man,
Alive,
Aware of his dependence,
Sentimental and intense.
A caring person—
Knowing how to give.
A being guided by
The Father—
Unafraid to live.

Involvement

Love given,
Risk;
Misunderstanding,
Rejection,
Loneliness, or
Acceptance.
Ultimately, sacrifice.
Risk.

Gratitude

For persons who say
At various times,
In meaningful ways,
 "I like you"—
  my thanks.

For persons whose tears
Will mingle with mine,
Who comfort my fears
 of failing—
  my thanks.

For people of God
So willing to give,
United in love,
 redemptive—
  my thanks.

Love Me

Love me
Not for what I do, but
For what I am—for me.
Love me whether I reflect
The strengths
Or weaknesses
Of you.
Give me warmth,
Not coverings.
Show me that I do exist,
Whether by anger
Or by smiles.
Care to give me more than
Just acknowledgment.
Care enough to
Love me!

19

A WOMAN RESPONDS

   ... TO HER INNER SELF

Commitment

Commitment grows
In choices, small
And sometimes even unaware.
It is more than promise.
More than beginning.
It is, perhaps, never to be sure.
Commitment is to
Endure.

Anger

She spoke,
And anger grew within
My fingers,
Closing them into my palms.
I sought to spit out
Slicing words
And to dismantle her
Facade.
My eyes were wide,
Impatient, and
My neck was tense
With self-control.
I would have gladly cast aside
My seething calm
To feel relief from fury's fire.
With no time
To wait for reason,
I was torn to burst—
Perhaps destroy—
Or hold my tongue
And live a lie.

Nourishment

To feed on only memories is naught.
Tears will quench not thirst, and
Past endeavors are not bread.
Consuming retrospect will serve to quell
The appetite for giving,
Which would once again restore
The spirit's strength.

Freedom

I am a balloon on a string.
Jauntily I bob and bounce,
Yet reluctance holds that string.
From without I look so gay,
From within I may explode,
Bursting my illusory shell.
Will I jerk and bob and toss,
And never really soar?
Can I free myself and float
Into the currents of life's sky?

Shell

When I crawl into
My shell of fear
I am become
Destroyed.
I measure words
Until I no longer
Dare to speak.
I hold the delicate
Glass of joy
So firmly
That it shatters,
Breaking into a thousand
Pieces of regret.
I look back in sadness
And I fail to respond
To the call of coming
Possibilities.
It is dark within
My shell.
And until I can
Push free,
Death is not the future—
Death is every day.

Doldrum

All day long
I have been thinking
Of the past and
Of tomorrow
And of me
And of me.
And I'm tired of that someone
Looking at me
In the mirror.
I do not want to see her
Though she will not
Cease to be.
I am tired.
I am weary.
I will sleep and then be free.

Praise

Living without recognition
Is to never live at all.
It is in meeting praise and conflict
That we know identity.
But if brief and fleeting praise
Becomes the bread sustaining me,
I shall find an empty void
When other persons pass away.
I must know and build my strengths
Within the bounds of given self.

Fear

Fears
    drip in the hidden mind,
Eroding every level plain,
And growing to a stream of thought
Which can consume all calm.
As we submit to their decay,
A river of anxiety
Churns murky waves of discontent
To immobility.
Yet, this is Man;
Dependent and inclined to drown
In his self-centered misery,
Afraid—
Unless he finds, through other men,
That of God which casts out fear—
Love.

Struggle

I was running, frantic,
In between life's raindrops,
Trying to arrive, unscathed;
Fearful I might slip and stumble
Into some unpleasant puddle—
Weary and restrained.

Then I slowed my steps
And walked.
I felt the coolness of the raindrops.
I was trusting—drenched in living.
And I did not fall—
I loved it all!

Direction

In love
And hate
To know the truth of what
I am.

To see the depths of hurt—
And mend the damage
I create.
To hear the messages, unsaid,
That cry in human hearts
And souls.
To freely yield forgiveness
And to welcome opportunities
To love.

This is my purpose, my being.

Suspended

Sometimes I want to
Stop my life
And hold on to these persons
And these moments
That I cherish.
Keep alive my loved ones,
Always hold my little boys upon my lap,
Look up at the sky
Through apple blossoms and new elm growth,
Smell the smoke of burning autumn leaves,
And not move on.
Life is confusing.
I would hurry into new adventures,
But I would stand still.

Motivation

There are forces in this life
Which drive us on—
Compelling.
One such force, a sense of duty.
Another, unrelenting guilt.
Yet another, the gift of ego;
Powerful humanity.
But the greatest force of all is
Love.

Rebirth

Is it possible that
Within one short moment
One can look at the
Graceful beauty of a tree
And *see* it?
Be sensed to the song of
Birds
And *hear* them?
Open the heart of
Love
And give?
Or was the beauty,
The harmony,
The glory
Always there—
    Waiting . . .
      Waiting . . .
        For the morning?

A WOMAN RESPONDS

... TO NATURE

Spring

Spring has come!
My muscles want to stretch,
Reaching far into the world of freedom.
The wind whirls away my introspection and
Sends me sailing into fresh pursuit of life.
Each new touch of sunshine
Slips in and gently erases my discontent.
Inspired once again to see God everywhere,
My spirit is engulfed
By his living presence.

Lovely Flower

Lovely flower, you live so beautifully.
You freely drink of both the sun and rain.
Although you know the storm could quickly crush
    you,
You burst forth and you do not shrink away.
You do not grow puffed up at blossoms' beauty;
You know they are dependent on your stem.
Yours is a calm surrender to the evening,
And to the day when life shall cease to be.
Would that I had spirit such as yours is.
Lovely flower, you live so beautifully.

Summer Storm

Humid heat rests heavily over all, with
Clouds churning in rapid change.
Children scurry indoors and
Doors blow shut behind them.
Eyes peer skyward, searching for the future—
Gray sky,
Gray air,
A burst of wind and an ominous feeling of
   powerlessness.
Trees begin to bend graceful arms
In a violent thrashing of leaves and twigs.
Rushing sounds fill one's head and
Heighten fears of hell itself.
Paper and the world's folly blow swiftly by
For all to see their temporal soul.
Rain dashes briefly against all that is solid
And Nature hurls her darts at her unwilling
   target—
The world.

Wild Poppies

Let me see
A field of wild poppies
And bachelor buttons—
Drooping red and
Straight-up blue
Against the slender, common green,
And I will feel free.

Rain

Rain, beat on the earth!
Drive away its ugly form.
Wash man's world of selfish striving.

Rain, fall on my fingers.
Lightly refresh their weariness.
Caress my face with newness of vision.

Rain, open the heavens!
Release your waters of Time.
Yield your tears of grace and forgiveness.
Lead us again to the Sun.

Autumn

Swirling smoke of burning leaves
spins a warm cocoon of
fragrant memories
around me.

Crispness of the changing world
excites my consciousness
with childlike zest and
wonderment.

Thoughtful in the tranquil rain,
or singing in the sun,
I celebrate life's
symphony.

January Rain

A freezing January rain,
Like an artisan glass blower,
Created an elegant world of glass
Transcendent to the skill of mortal man.

Trees, like gigantic crystal chandeliers
Arched gracefully over quiet streets,
Brightening the night—
Shining in scattered brilliance in the light of day.
The sun
Darting in and out between branches and twigs,
Left behind a trail of sparkling sundust.

Young trees and bushes were bent
In aching backstrain
Under the gaudy weight of the translucent veneer.
Worldly wires were ornamented in icicle patterns.

And the eyes of rushing, restless man
Stopped
To gaze in incredulous fixation
At the wonder of God and rain.

A WOMAN RESPONDS

. . . TO SOCIETY

Window Pane

Have you looked into the eyes
  of the ghetto teacher?
Eyes squinting against the
      NOISE in the old halls
      that whomps up and down
      in magnified echoes
      over and over and over.

Tired eyes
      looking for enough crayons
      and a different way—
      a new design for learning
      where the leader follows.

Strained eyes
      seeing unending needs
      and thirty-five persons
      smashed into
         one
         big
      movement of arms and legs.

The eyes watch over a world
      where "no" is not enough
      and "maybe" is everyday
        to children of uncertainty,
      and time
         time
         time could help—
         but time
         costs
      and no one pays.

Conscience

I had this dress I didn't like
Anymore.
I gave it to the clothing drive.
"Poor people need it."
It was convenient for me
And for my conscience.

But today—
Today I saw my dress
Upon a woman on the street,
Alive!
My conscience was not easy
Anymore.

Money? Money *does* buy
Peace of mind and
Self-respect for many.
But not for me
Anymore.

I cannot let my
Dress and coins be
Second-hand
Excuses
For a real gift—
Me.

Understanding

Because I've never known a
Gnawing hunger,
I may never understand the
Deep despair to which
It drives you.
    But I can try,
    For I can see within the hollow
    Shell of saddened eyes
    Your fading hope of help.

I may never know again
The anguish of a mind which
Seeks to read
The simplest word
And does not know it.
    But I can try,
    Because I can remember
    What it was
    To want to learn,
    And have no help from
    Teacher.
When duty
Grows oppressive,
I can get away to

Shops or to the lake,
So I may not grasp
Your desperate need for freedom.
   But I can try,
   For I can sympathize
   With what must be
   An uninspiring,
   Endless road of
   Children's cries and
   Self-denial.

I can try and
I *will* try to capture
Your frustration,
And to help you
Set it free.

Alcoholic

A moment of fear,
A sip of wine,
And reality escapes into
False confidence—
Alienation from
Truth
And family
And self—
From one brief moment
Of fear.

Futility

Cities
    confusion
        concrete
dirt
    clocks
        numbers
            trapped!

Masses—no meaning,
People—not persons.
Wandering, lost in a suppressive cage.

Where am I?
Who am I?
Dear God! Is this life?

Drama

He stands alone
Wavering in the
Middle of the street—
A derelict,
Center stage,
In a long coat
Aged brown—
His, by acquiescence
To the generosity of
Goodwill.
He gestures broadly
To his audience
In cars which stop
To watch him.
His garbled speech is
Tangled in his unshaven face,
Devoid of mask.
A soliloquy of despair.

Soul

Of course you may scrub—
Teach if you like.
Pay, even.
It helps us.
But that will not be your
Answer.
You
Are your answer.
You will begin to help
When you begin to
Feel "brother."
And I will know when
You
Has begun.

Farewell

I do not understand this war.
I only know
That finally
It touches me and
I can only pray
You will survive, my son.
Death is real,
And now I must acknowledge it.
Now I must rely
On trust
As you step forward to the task
That nations and their people
Need assign you.
God bless you.
I will miss you, son.

A WOMAN RESPONDS

... TO LOVE

Surrender

Your tenderness sifts gently into
All my being,
Smoothing my ruffled reluctance,
And nestling in my heart.
Touched by the promise of love,
I grow warm and eager to embrace you.
Kiss me, dear one.
Kiss my hand and kiss my lips.
Turn my chin and I shall
Gaze into the everlasting eyes
Of love.
Suddenly my yearning grows
Into a flaming passion.
I am yours.
Thank God!

Love

My fears begin to melt away
And trust accepts the mystery.
Eyes can meet,
Hands reach out,
And I am warm in your embrace.
There is fullness in a bond
Which comfortably rests secure.
At last I know that I can give,
And I can welcome love—with you.

Joy

He loves me!
He cares.
I shudder at the magnitude
To which my spirit now can rise.
I am at once
Above the crowd,
Transformed by his
Unbounded gift.
Sustained by his respect and trust,
I joy to share my happiness.
Ah! Such beauty—
Being loved!

Lovers' Farewell

Lovers stand
Facing opposite directions
Shoulder to shoulder—
Afraid to touch
Or look into each other's eyes.
Aware that any
Hesitation
Will grow into a hopeless
Grasp at dreams.
They speak,
Unable to express the moment.
They pause,
They part.
And walking toward their separate suns,
They weep.

Separation

I shall leave, my love.
But I shall not pretend the trees
Are green and new
As when your magic fashioned spring.
I shall leave, my love.
And branches will be bare and bleak,
The winter cold,
As lonely days await the spring.

But spring will come
Because I've known a warmth and glow
In knowing you.
Because you gave unselfishly,
I know that I can also give,
And I shall one day live again,
Though now I leave you, love.

Hold Me

Today I am discouraged—
Hold me.
I need your strength to comfort me—
Hold me.
Wrap compassion's arm around me.
Numb my nerve ends
To the sting of failure's darts.
I can try again,
Refreshed,
If only you enfold me.
Hold me.

Realization

I cling to the
Moving music as a
Song I cherish begins
To fade.

A thread of tension
Lingers on the edge
Of my feeling self
As I remember
You.

A tiny, wistful sigh,
Unwillingly emitted,
Surprises me and
My apparent calm becomes
Excitement.

I am again astonished
By the power of your
Love.

A WOMAN RESPONDS

. . . TO MARRIAGE

John

How would I suffice
Without you?
Who would calm my anger,
Overlook my pride?
Who would trust
Implicitly,
Encourage me
When I falter?
Who would listen and respect?
Who would love as
You have loved?

The Eve of a Marriage

Laughter of love
Complements the nostalgia of
Memories.
The awareness of decision
Enriches the excitement of the
Future.
And the world prepares
To welcome a union
Blessed.

Renewal

Once more let me adore you;
Look on you with eyes
Quite blinded by the
Brilliance of love.
Let the expectation
Of fulfillment
Once more dull all senses
To the cares of life.
Then I gladly will return
To routine living,
New.

Unity

To be consoled,
To be caressed,
To know that someone waits for you,
Is to be blessed.
To have a need which you can fill,
To be forgiven of self-will.
To share, to live—
To be one.

A WOMAN RESPONDS

. . . TO MOTHERHOOD

Pregnancy

Within my body grows a child,
I feel him move,
I know him.
I feed him with my every breath,
My body and my thought.
I wait to hold him in my arms,
As now I hold him in my womb.
My heart embraces what he is,
And what his hopes and life may be.
Within my body grows a child,
An everlasting miracle.

Growing

Sometime between today and yesterday
Our little baby grew into a boy.
Curiosity excited independence,
Discovery demanded new self-will.
Love expression pours on us, unbridled,
But his own needs cry to be fulfilled.
Reluctantly we recognize his selfhood.
We struggle with desires to keep him small.
We try to balance discipline and freedom.
We strive to keep our aspirations fair.
We see the man emerging here before us,
We see the mystery of change and life.

My Sparrow

My child, a little sparrow,
Hops up beside me—
    Chirping, chirping.
Snuggling in a nest of
    Love which I would have
    Protect him.
Bobbing in delight
    To see the sunlight of the day.
Fluttering his frail wings
    As he tries to reach new heights—
    Proud, undaunted,
    Unafraid.
Coy and cheerful,
    Swooping down in mischief,
    Mingling his laughter
    With my own.
My little sparrow!
My sheer delight!

A Baby

A surge of joy
Captures me as my son first
Begins to love.
When one day he is
Smiling back at me—
Laughing with abandon at the
Little games we play;
His small, wet mouth
Nuzzling my cheek or chin,
His head nestled into my shoulder
During a lullaby.
Here is his love, learned,
And now shared.
Here is God—giving.
And so begins my eternal thanks.

A Child

A child is small.
He must look up
To see where we would have him go,
To learn what we would have him know
And in our posture
We become quite tall.

A child grows.
He looks at life and us
With his own meaning,
His uniqueness,
And he challenges our stance,
For we must change.

Would we be tallest?
Keep him looking up
And never growing?
Can we let go?
Can we be honest—
Meet the person
Face to face?

A WOMAN RESPONDS

...TO LITTLE THINGS

The Farm

I would visit the farm
And perhaps they wondered
Why I came.
I was afraid to ride
The horses fast—
But I loved the hickory woods
Where horses went.
I did not have the
Gay abandon to enjoy
The hay loft or the muddy fields.
But I liked the house;
The old brick house was strong.
    The back porch smelled of
    Washing soap.
    The rooms were large—
    They echoed and
    The mirror went from the
    Ceiling to the floor.
    The kitchen was the best.
    People liked to be there,
    Cooking, eating, talking.
The people were the
Reason that I came.
Their anger was loud,

Their kindness, direct.
Their laughter was long
Until we would have to leave the table
In tears.
Their love was real—
It showed.
And one day I looked up and saw
Across the table
The brother who had been there
All the time.
He was smiling;
The boy whom I first loved
And kissed.
Often I return to the
Shaded, quiet memories
Of the farm.

Poetry

Within the heartbeat of a thought
Pulses every person's dream.
A poem tells the meaning,
Saves the memory,
And the thought lives on.

Perspective

Pressing problems
Melt beneath my iron.
Wrongs wash clean in
Warm suds of the day.
Irritations neatly fold
Within the darkness of a drawer.
Children's cries
Are dusted into air.
Help me, Lord, to find these satisfactions
In the daily tasks which I pursue.
All a home
Reflects the light of mother.
Warmth, responding to
The living God.

My Room

It was a good room.
Where I could lie in bed and
Sometimes see the moon among the trees.
Where I could be annoyed
Or charmed
By noisy sparrows in the morning.
Where I could hear the muffled sounds
Of cars in winter snow
In the street below.
It was a room where I could cry,
Or dream,
Or rest in stillness.
It was a good room.

Daydream

Reach for a heaven—
Candy floss,
Pink champagne,
A train ride to bells ringing,
And roses.
Sparkling new love,
Confetti and
Spring.
A moment's escape
From reality.

A WOMAN RESPONDS

 ... TO THE PAINS OF LIFE

Human Sandcastle

A sandcastle:
Built with grains of youth-concept,
Cemented with water and vanishing creme.
Minarets of new fashions
Painted with rouge,
Overbalance the foundation
Of no-future.

The structure begins to slide
Away into the sea
Of age.
Hands, hasty to rebuild,
Cannot outrace the tide.
The heat of afternoon
Dries up the spirit
Long since left behind
In the morning-present building
Of a sandcastle.

Divorce

Divorce
Divides—
But it only separates
Two.
Friends,
Family,
Memories and yesterdays
Remain:
Somehow disjointed—
Severed,
Yet tied.
It is a difficult resolve,
Divorce.

Reality

A tear of separation brimming in
    the eye of love,
Foreshadow of the pains of life amid
    the joy of birth,
Sounds of kindness falling on deaf ears
    or hardened hearts,
The everpresent tragedy within
    the beautiful.

Restraint

A moment's gaze is fuel
Enough to swell the fire
Of discontent,
When love which must remain
Untouched, yet burns.
Laughter shared becomes
A tremble, wavering
The tranquil stance,
Revealing depths of passion
Unforeseen.
Love restrained torments
The souls of them who yearn
To yield, fulfilled.
They search for meaning in
The anguish they endure.

Traffic Accident

The night is cut through by a
Rolling, jarring noise,
Enclosing me like thunder
With its muffled explosion.
Glass,
Broken body,
Shattered life—and death
Outside my window.
With trembling hand I dial police
And turn in deep despair to
Watch the spectacle outside.
Flashbulbs pry.
They stir the night like beads of lightning.
Autos stop—and people come
To peek inside the twisted ruin
Of what once had been a car.

> Go away, you people!
> Go away! You do not know him.
> Curiosity, sensation—
> Let him die in privacy!
> Did you doubt that death could happen?
> Just what is it you would see?
> In that twisted body there remains
> No meaning—
> Not even in the flowing blood—
> Unless it is the sadness it evokes in me
> For persons left to mourn.

A child's set of encyclopedias
Strewn among the wreckage,
Stare up in isolation at the crowd.
I feel sick way deep inside me,
And the knot within my stomach aches.
I wonder if the man who died
Has had a family?
Who must tell them?
Who will help them?
What of those now left alone?
I am glad they do not see the sight
Now laid before me.
How unhappy it has made me—
What a tragedy for them!
My brow still furrowed,
Spirit weakened,
I can only walk away
And ponder.
Life goes on, but for a moment
Life has stood still.

Tragedy

"Mother, Daddy—can I say it?
Will you try to understand?
Mother, Daddy! Oh, I'm pregnant!
God forgive me, it is true.
Once I loved him.
Love is gone.
But a child now lives within me.
Oh, please love me. Help me, please!"

Mixed within a wail of sorrow
Disbelief engulfs our soul.
Am I guilty? I, the parent?
Is redemption possible?
Disappointment, shattered visions,
Memories of innocence,
Overwhelm the sense of reason,
Tear at hearts who love so much.
To know and then to say goodbye—
An offspring never to be held!
To see a daughter's agony
When birth can be so beautiful.
Perhaps the human heart can never
Understand this piece of life.
Perhaps the only resolution
Is found within the grace of God.

Moving

Forty years we lived here—
Forty years.
We planted all the flowers.
We watched our pine trees grow.
Peter made the birdhouse.
Peter cannot be here anymore.

I don't know how that old furniture
Will look in the new house,
But the work of settling in
Will ease the sting of leaving here.
I wish . . .
I cannot wish—I must go on.
But, forty years . . . .

Lonely Child

Lonely child,
Forgotten,
Predisposed to fail
In ventures new.
Wherein lies the source
Of his despair?
Rejected? When?
Unlovely? Why?
A life already robbed
Of joyous meaning.
How much giving will be needed
To redeem the
Lonely child?

Call for Help

I stand as if in stagnant,
Clinging mud.
I sense that I must
Lift my foot.
I am unable.
Though I strain all
My energy and mind,
I cannot focus on
A task.
My arm is heavy,
Pulling on my shoulders
Until my neck and
Head begin to ache.
The ache does not
Subside,
But grows into a giant
Which swallows up the
Room and air around me.
I cannot run,
Nor can I hide,
Nor can I begin to see
A light.
I am sick.
In whom can I confide?

Hospital Stay

My son is gone.
His room, an empty room
Filled with unbreathed air
And memories.
A bib upon a chair,
A voice I cannot hear,
Save distantly . . . .
A wish I cannot fill,
The morning hours—too still
And unresponsive.
I long to chatter with him—
End the thinking
And the unavailing
Wondering.
Bring him back to me—
To hold,
To love,
To give.
Please, bring him home again.

A WOMAN RESPONDS

. . . TO DEATH

Sorrow

"Oh!
My baby, my baby, my baby,"
I cried as I rocked his limp body in my arms,
And felt the measureless distance
Between life and Life.
Tears streamed over memories.
Weak senses grasped reality.
And for a moment, meaning was lost.
Visions, virtues, anticipated victories,
Melted into endless sorrow.
"My baby! My baby is dead."

*"Sorrow" is dedicated to
    Dewey and Lyn*

Wondering

I can't deny the
Truth of death.
I can't avoid
Reality.
Nor can I face myself
Unknown,
And lost in some
Nonentity.
Perhaps in others
I can find
A sense of immortality.
My child, perhaps,
Can carry forth
Myself and future
Destiny.
No; somehow I will
Learn to live
With life's most grave
Uncertainty.
I'll seek the something
Bigger
Than the mere
Existent life of me.

Childlike Faith

We were walking in the alley
When Bobby announced,
"A dead bird."
Sarah stopped to see,
Then we went on.
Children better
Comprehend death
In its true perspective,
For they see it as a fact,
And have no fear.

Grief

Tears will not bring back
Our daddy.
Tears can only wash away
The sting that lies
Behind the eyes and
Deep within the heart.
Tears will not erase the ache,
Nor change the fact
That he could die.
But I will cry . . . and cry . . . and cry.

Funeral

The long black car,
Grandma in the front seat,
All of us behind her
Traveling
To say goodbye to Mother.
The thread of perfume someone wears
Becomes the fabric of
A shroud
Which will drop over me
Whenever I should once more
Chance to meet its fragrance.
Mascara smudges and
Awkward hands clutch at gloves
And the unknown
Which lies ahead,
On a day when only yesterday
Seems real.
Hope within the
Voices of the many who have come
Because they care,
Will sustain the long tomorrows
Which will surely be.

A WOMAN RESPONDS

...TO FAITH

Christmas

Wistfully I wished for snow
To add to the sentimental glow
Of Christmas.
"Make the dreary world
White and clean for the Newborn," I said.

Our Christmas Eve was wrapped
In the cozy atmosphere of tradition.
Then it snowed!
I smiled.

I took a walk that night
Among our inner-city streets.
No snow could hide the loneliness;
No covering up of needs.
The snow fell,
But I wept.

Then I saw
That the Child did not expect to find
A clean, white world.
To cover up with white is the scheme
Of men who do not wish to
See.
Jesus came not to hide the world
But to change it.
And Jesus works through
Me.

Reformation

Tall, the spire—
Stretching high into the realm.
Music enchants the worshiper
And floats into the air around.
Stained glass
Calms the spirit in the pew.

Tall, the spire—
Shadowing the lives outside the church.
Music does not permeate the
Brick and enter life.
Stained glass only shades the light,
It does not set it free.

God, oh, let us liberate!
Throw open all the doors.
Send out the voice,
And yes, the heart.
Give the Gospel—
Share the Life.

Communion

Together—
Bowed and kneeling,
Equal in stature
Under the hand
Of the Redeemer.
Blessed,
Forgiven,
Grateful.

Sanctuary

Blue, misty light
Quiet
Peace
A moment apart
A sharing with God
Music
Reflection
Calm

Sanctuary

Snowflakes

We are snowflakes
Floating in the atmosphere of
Life.
Driven by the winds of Time,
    We alter course and drift.
Individually unique—
    Yet bound, universally.
Lovely forms,
    We can be cold.
Delicate,
    We can destroy.
White and pure as we begin,
Our journeys taint our
Destiny.
We are made to melt away,
    To vanish—
We do not endure.
Ultimately, each transformed;
Recreated, borne anew.

*I*ncarnation

Love,
Manifested in one man,
Makes my existence
Meaningful.
My span of life
Discovering
Myself—and Him
Who lived
Forgiveness.
Him:
Complete integrity.
Jesus,
     Love—
         Eternal.

*P*aradox

We indirectly seek to punish
Those whom God intends we love.
Words, and thoughtless lack of words,
Derange the destinies of men.
Knowing our self-interest,
We yet pursue a path of self—
Judging others' needs and purpose
By our own great needs' demands.
Our playing at omnipotence
Denies the strength of the Supreme,
And serves to make us only smaller;
Even more in need—of Him.

89

For Homemakers

Perhaps from where we find ourselves
It's difficult to see beyond today
Into Forever.
Our clothesbasket
   of aimless errands
Confuses opportunities for peace.
The clutter
   of our daily lives
Diffuses the redeeming rays of light.

The Church becomes the vehicle
Of God's plan and his love.
In it we find solitude.
The Spirit is in its saints.
Through it comes direction;
Purpose, in serving the world.
And in its substance we may find
Communion with the Truth—with God.

Anticipation

Like the grass, we wait for spring—
  Blanched white by our struggle,
  Entangled by our discontent, and
  Withered by the winter.
  Weary of our futile striving,
  Discouraged by our guilt and shame,
  Crushed beneath the treading feet of
  Man's indifference to man.
  Degenerates, we yearn for our
  Divine regeneration.
Then Easter comes,
And spring is born,
Hope, forgiveness, re-creation,
Growing grass—and green!

The Star

Spinning and swirling
Out of a massive creation of
Galaxies and glory,
Came a ray of light.
Ordained, it spun into
A focus of Truth.

Men stood still,
Awestruck at this wonder of the unknown.
Stirred by nature's splendor
And inspired to look beyond themselves,
They searched.
They found their essence
Couched in the familiar;
Wisdom, truth, majesty, and love
In a drafty cave
Among the lowly.

The light in a baby's cry
Illumined the dark,
Ascended above the tree,
Beyond the realm of men, and
Far into the reaches of the night.
And there evolved
A union of the Lights,
In a star.

Easter Garden

I am overcome by the
Fragrance of flowers and the
Phoniness of men who would
Enter church to
Escape the foul odors of life,
Imagining that garden air of
Uninvolvement could be
Fresh—
Or fragrant,
When the glory of Easter
Was a lily,
Made pure by
Struggling up through dirt,
Conquering the weeds and
 Blossoming, only after suffering in
The Garden of Gethsemane.

A WOMAN RESPONDS

... TO THE CREATOR

The Abundant Life

Waken all your spirit!
Let life's great adventure
Penetrate your shell.
Listen to the voices.
Share the common bond of
Pain and gladness.
Seize the moments for renewal.
Breathe deep the air of change
And love.
Live!

PS3563
A86F7   Mattison, Judith Nelson.
          From a woman's heart.   Illus. by The
       Stubstad.   Minneapolis, Augsburg Pub.
       [c1969]
          96 p.

          Poems.   O 7/87
                    1 4/09

       I. Title.